Fun-Schooling for
BEGINNERS
#6 "Do It Myself!"
JOURNAL
For The Littlest Fun-Schooler in the Family

The Thinking Tree, LLC
Created By:
Sarah Janisse Brown
FunSchoolingBooks.com

I AM LEARNING AND PLAYING!

All About Me
Sticker Collections
Preschool Word Games
Numbers Games
Learning Letters
Coloring Animals
Tracing
Logic
Coloring
Imagination
Drawing

Animal Alphabet

All About Me:

My Name:

_____

My Age: _____

My Birthday: _____

INSTRUCTIONS:

Let your child freely use the pages that they like best each day. If something is too hard, help and be an example. Play music or sing songs while your child is working in this book.

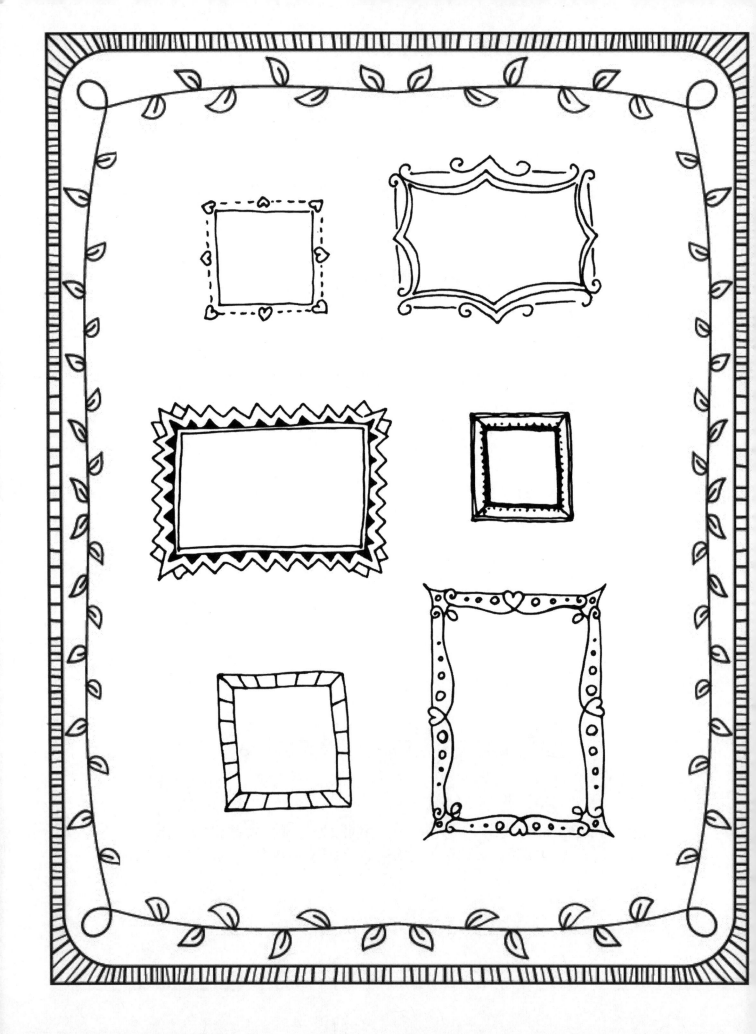

PART ONE
Letters, Numbers, Tracing & Coloring

A B C D E
F G h i J
K L M N
O P Q R S
T U V W
X Y Z

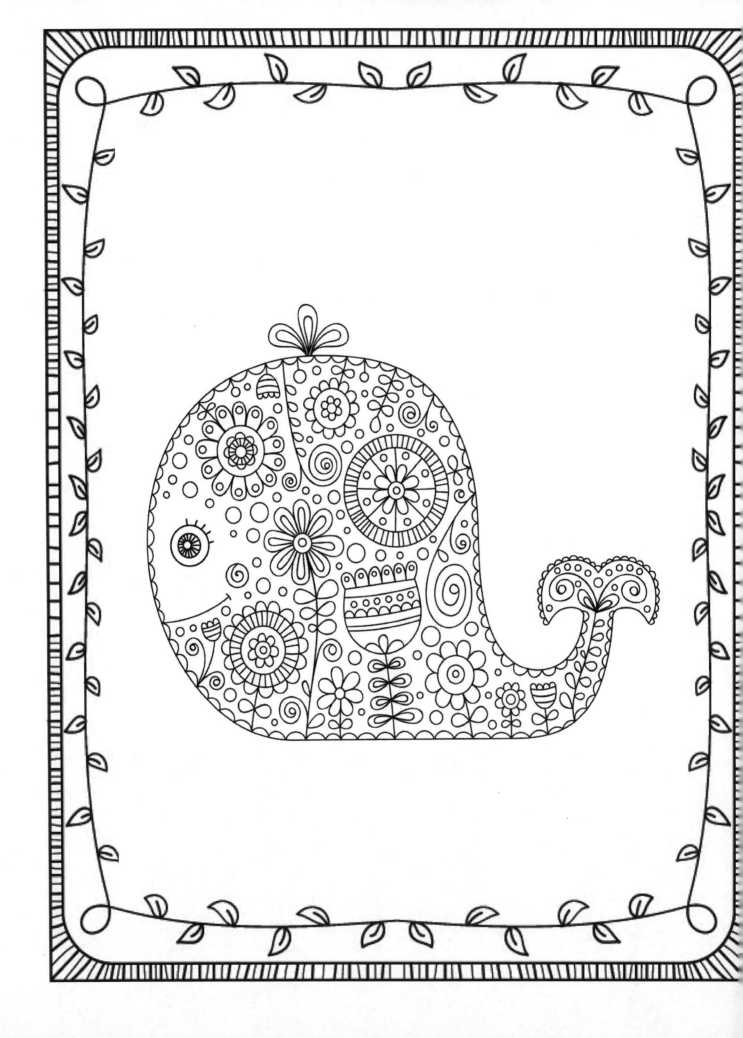

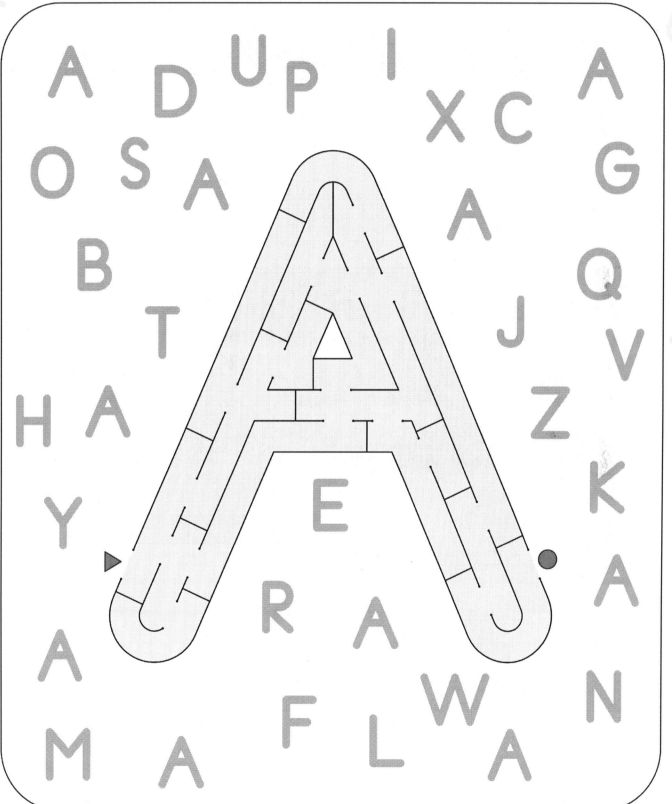

A B C D E F

G H I J K L

M N O P Q

R S T U V

W X Y Z

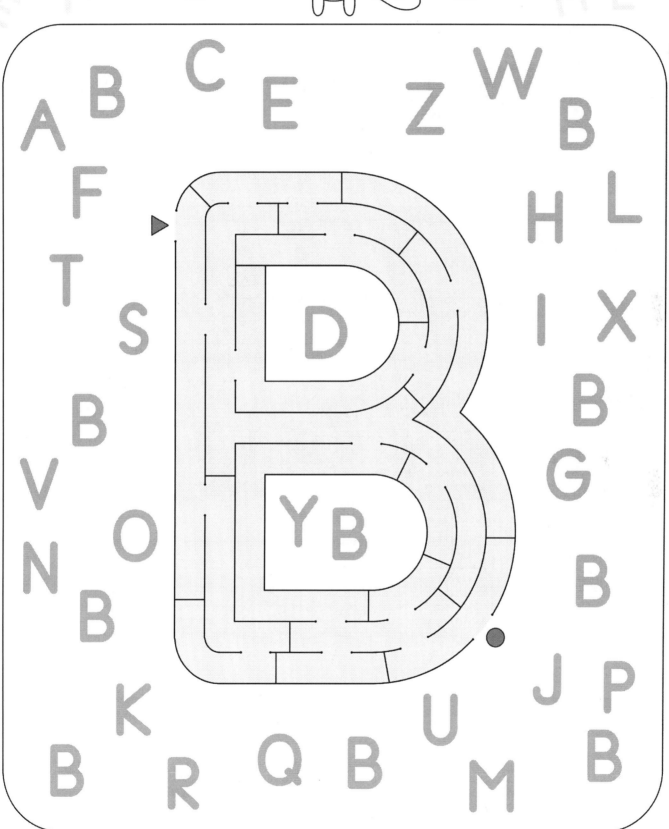

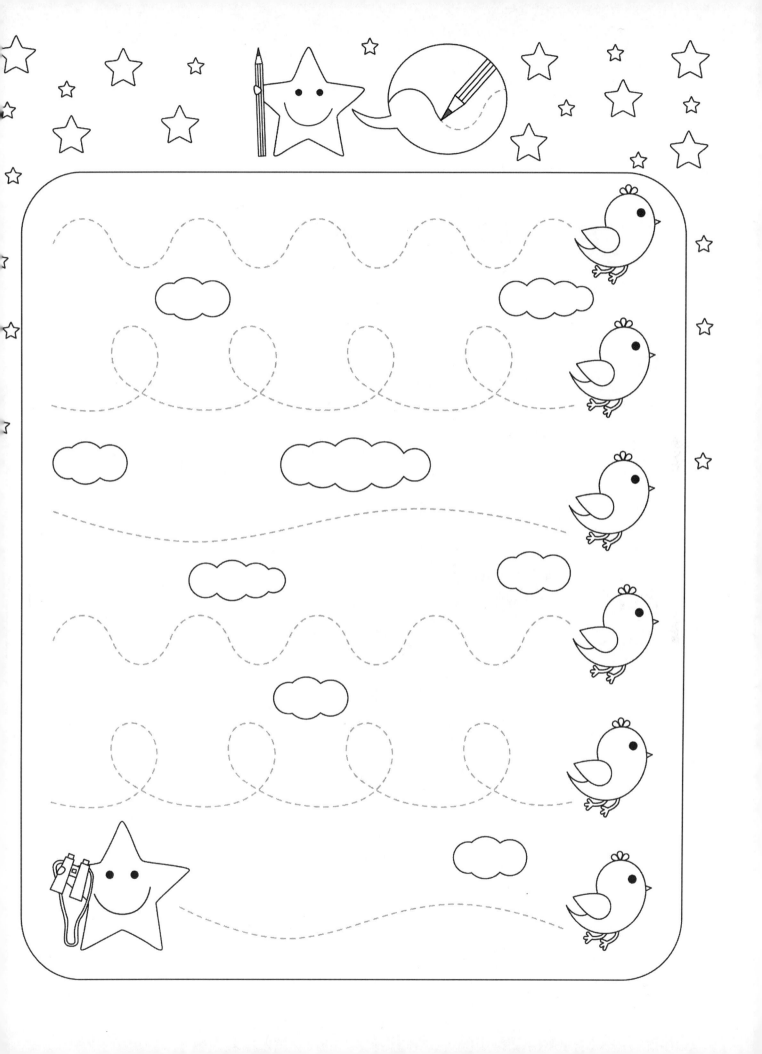

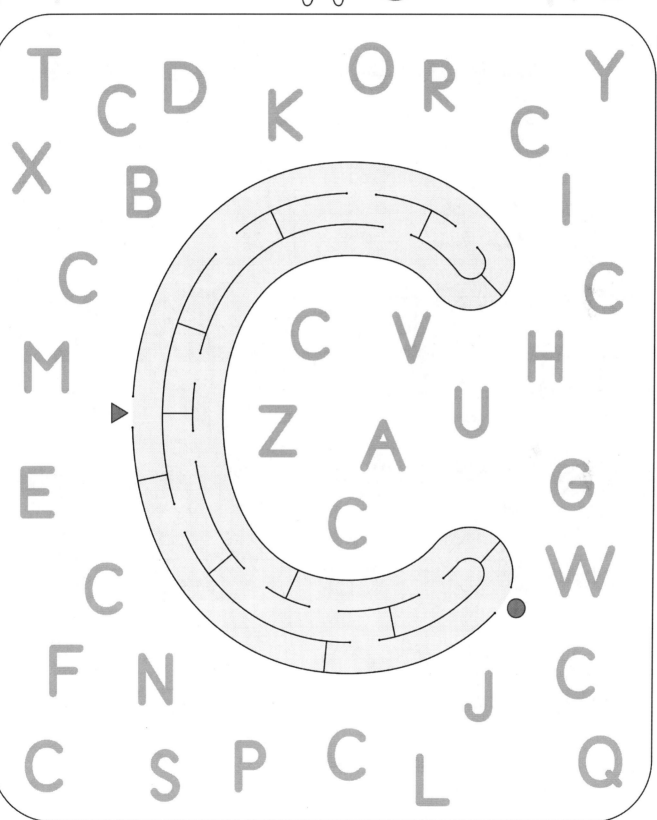

A B C D E F

G H I J K L

M N O P Q

R S T U V

W X Y Z

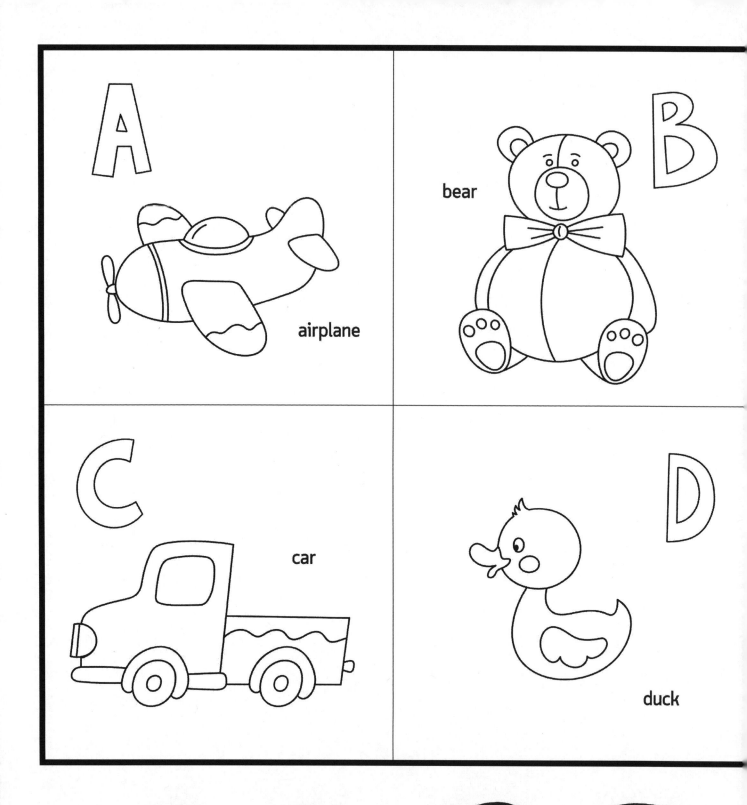

A
airplane

B
bear

C
car

D
duck

E

elephant

F

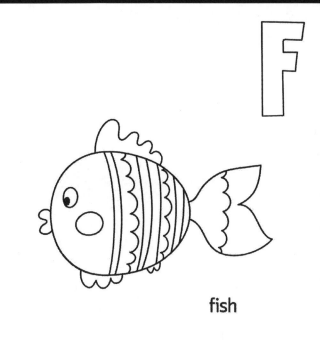

fish

G

goat

horse

H

 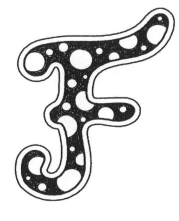  

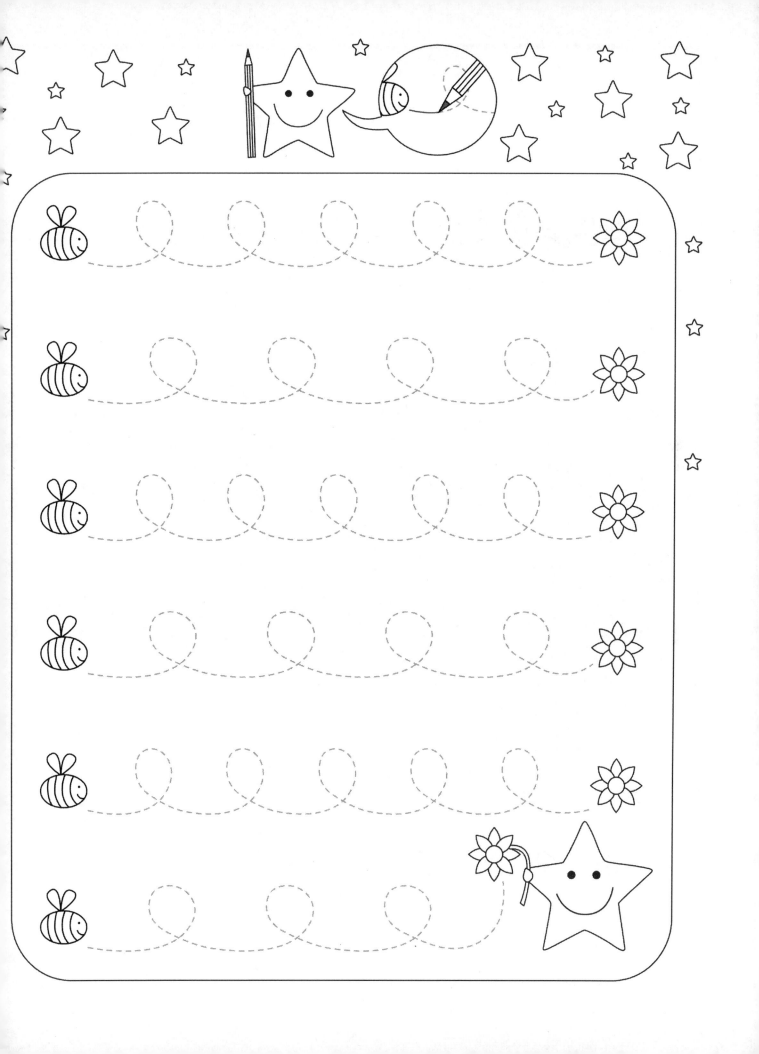

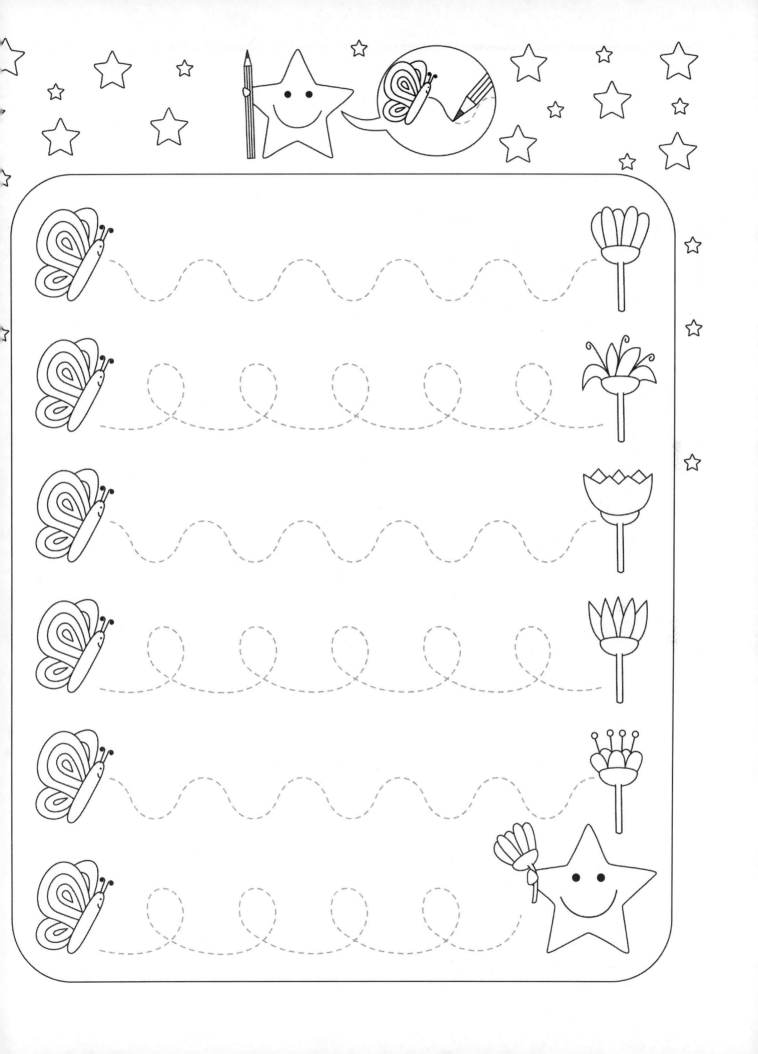

I

iguana

J

jellyfish

K

kite

L

lion

M

monkey

N

newt

O

owl

pig

P

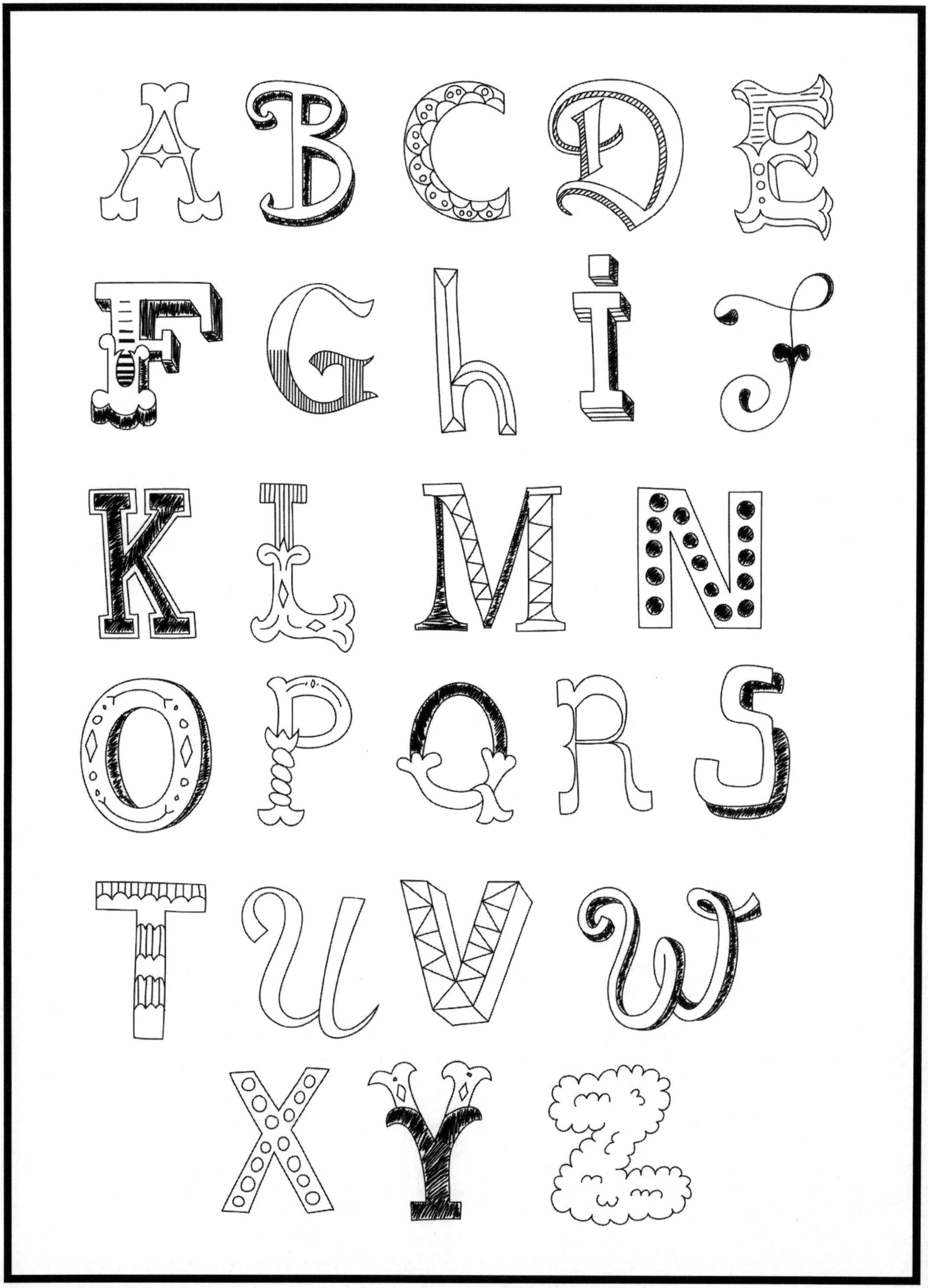

A B C D E
F G h i J
K L M N
O P Q R S
T U V W
X Y Z

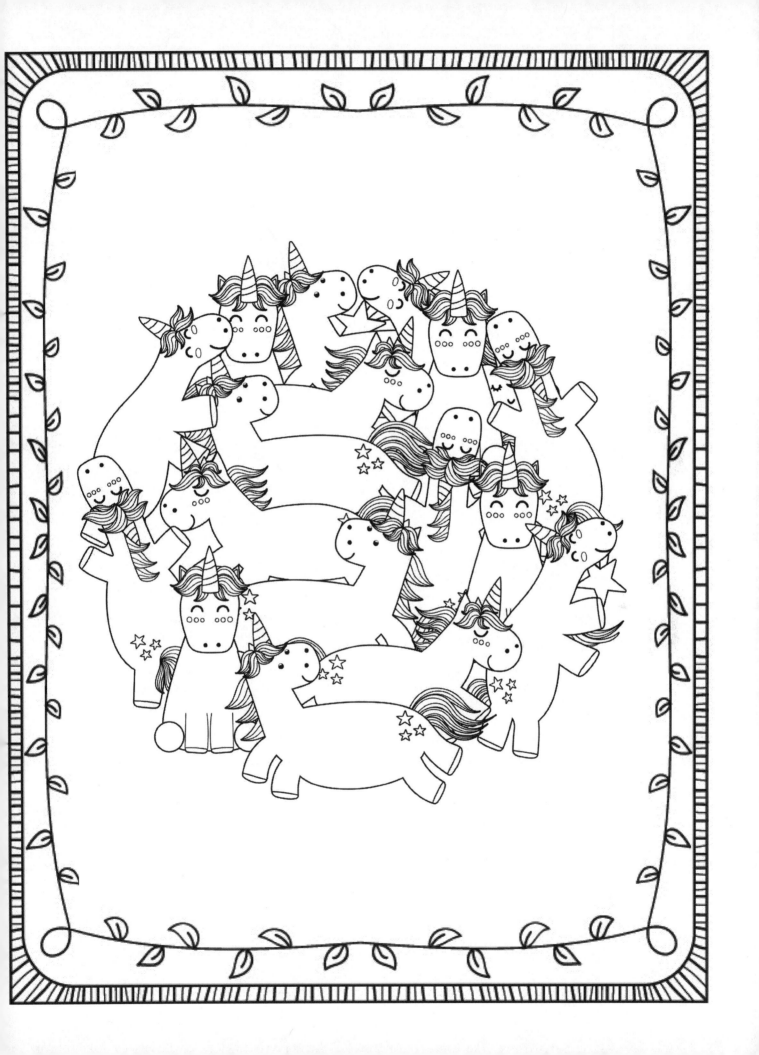

Q queen

R rabbit

S sheep

turtle T

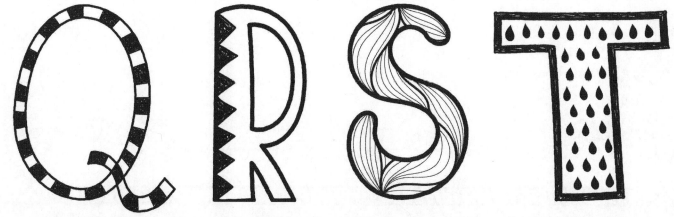

unicorn

Vampire bat

wolf

xylophone

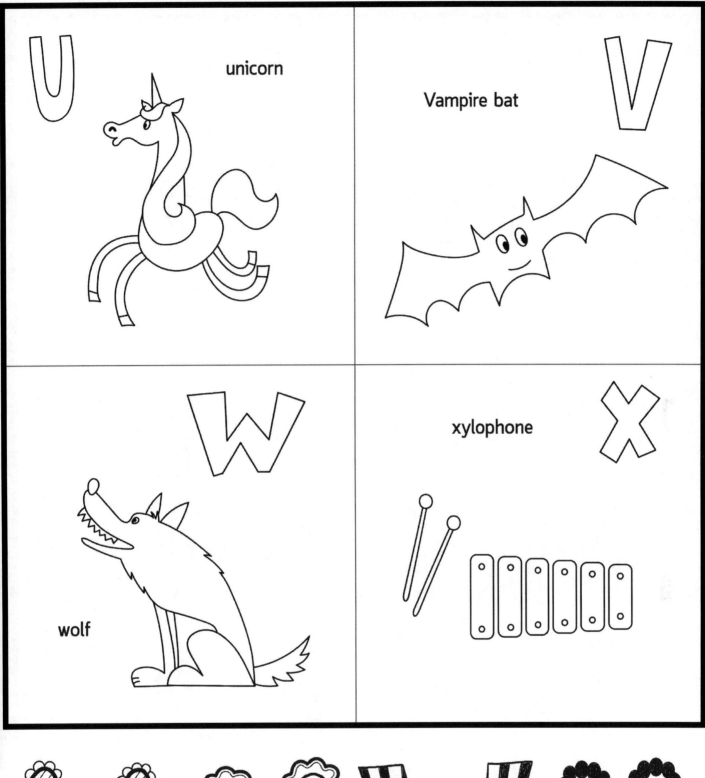

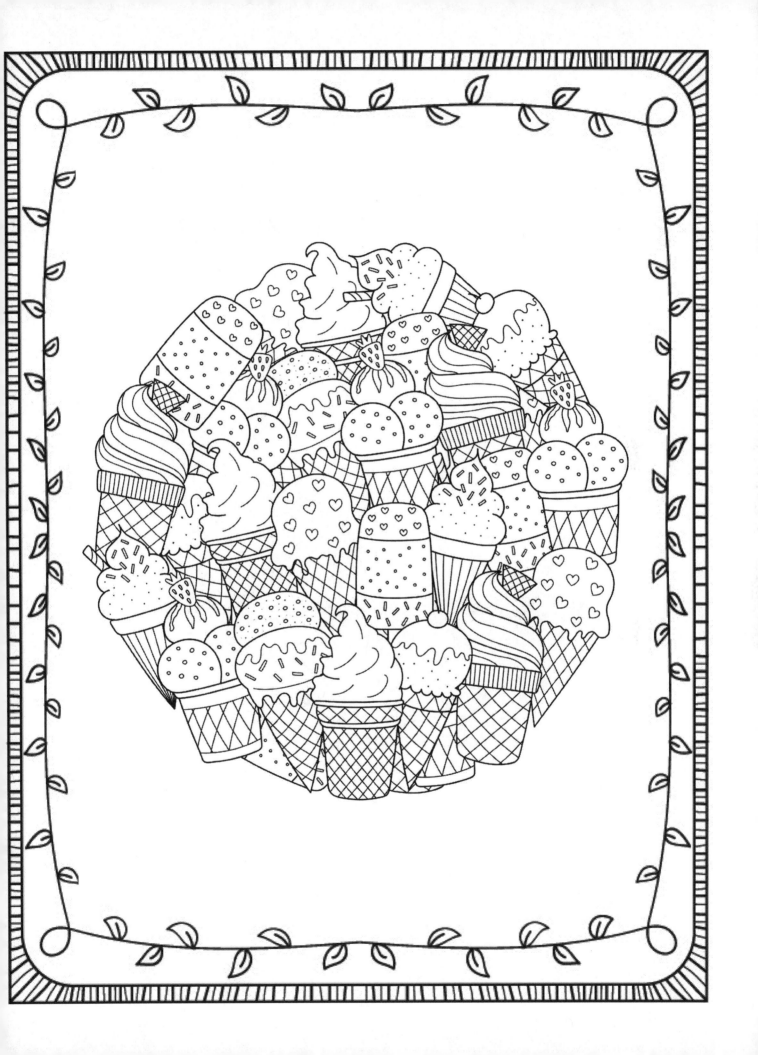

A B C D E F
G H I J K L
M N O P Q
R S T U V
W X Y Z

Y
yacht

Z

zebra

y z

ABCDEFGHIJKLM
NOPQRSTUVWXYZ

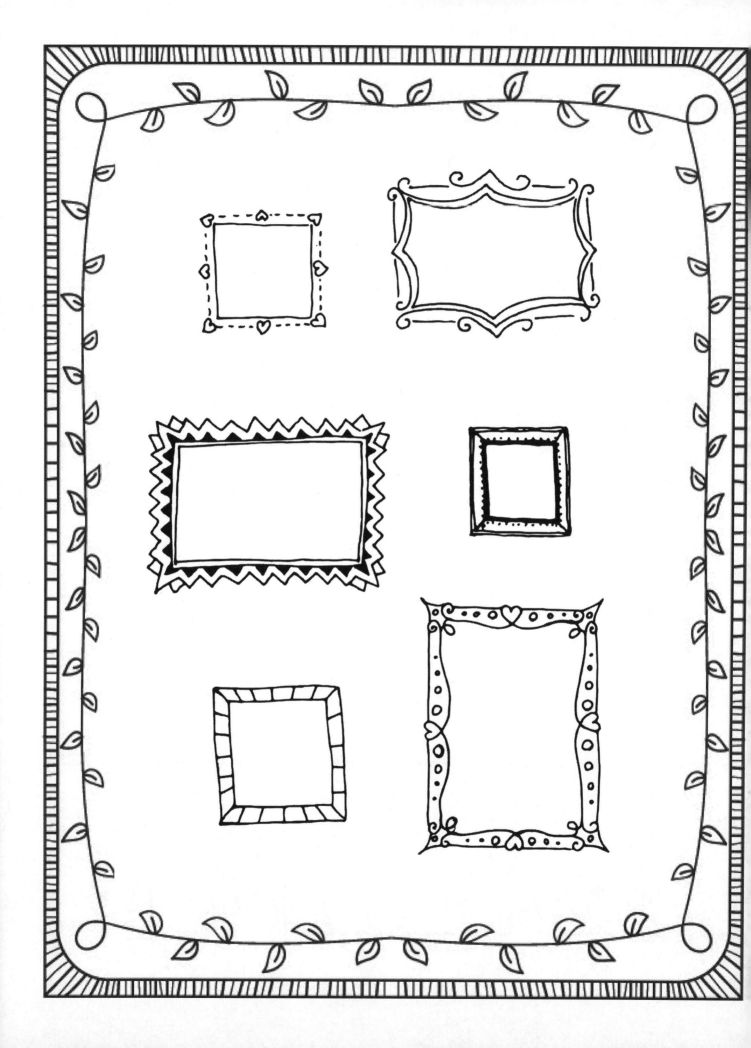

PART TWO
ALL ABOUT ME

Draw yourself here

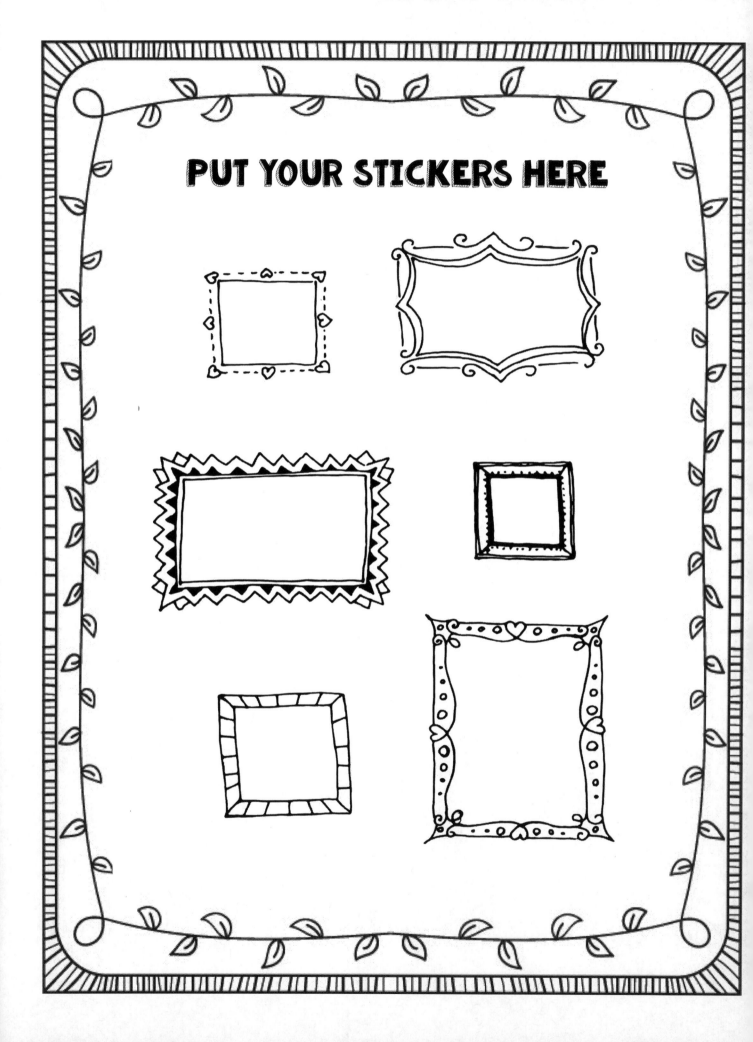

MY YARD

Draw things that
you see outside.

MY FAMILY

Draw your family

PUT YOUR STICKERS HERE

MY FAVORITE ANIMALS

MY HOUSE

MY ROOM

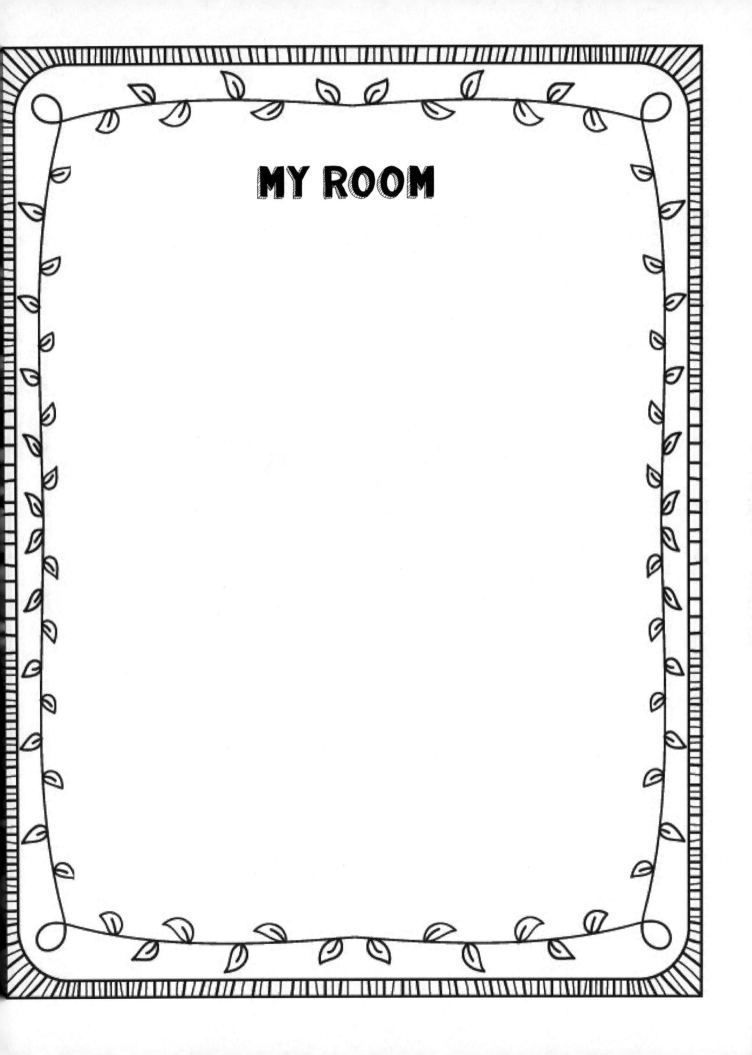

MY FACE

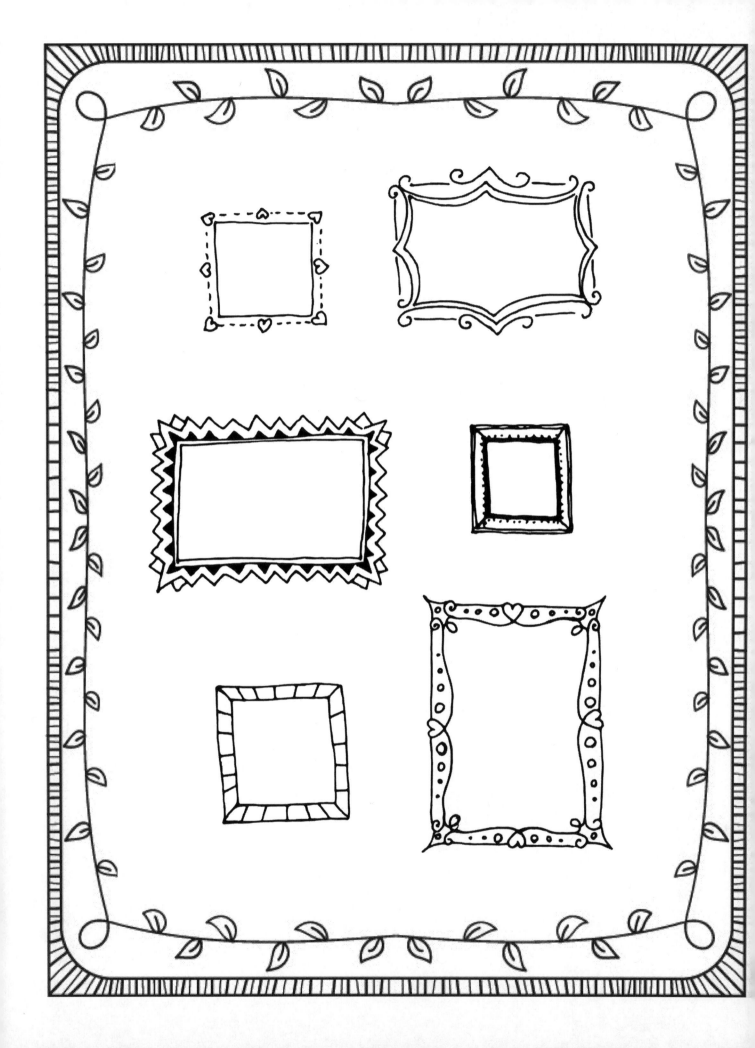

MY FAVORITE FOODS

MY FAVORITE COLORS

PUT YOUR STICKERS HERE

DRAW ANYTHING!

PUT YOUR STICKERS HERE

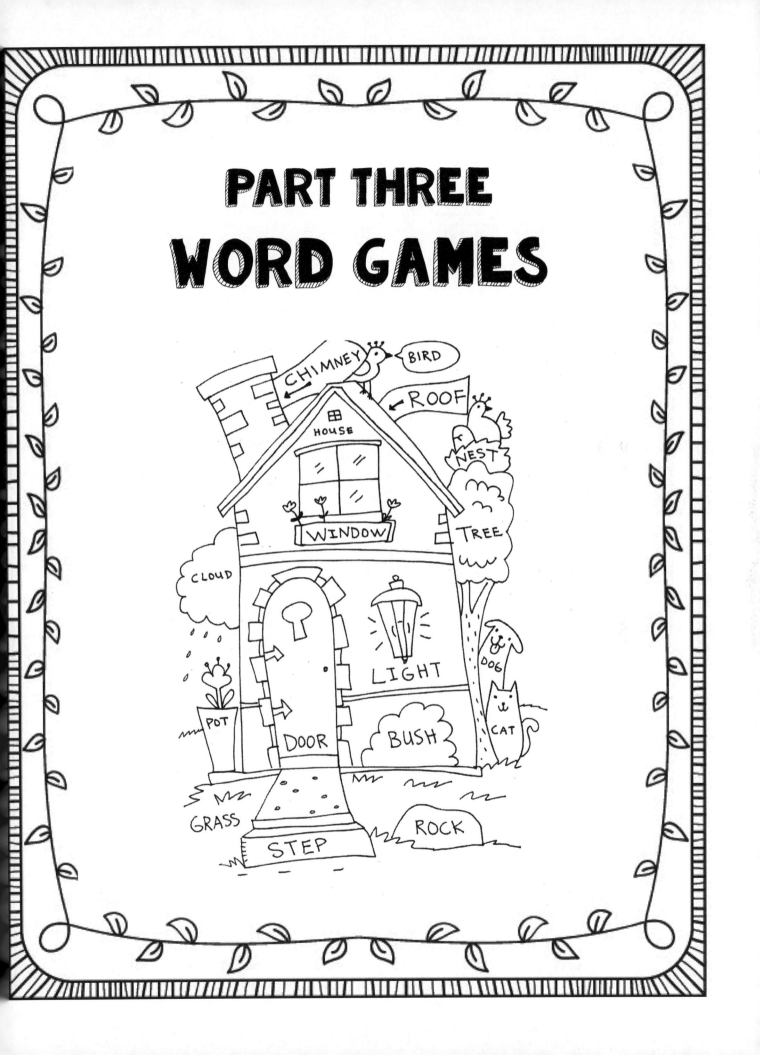

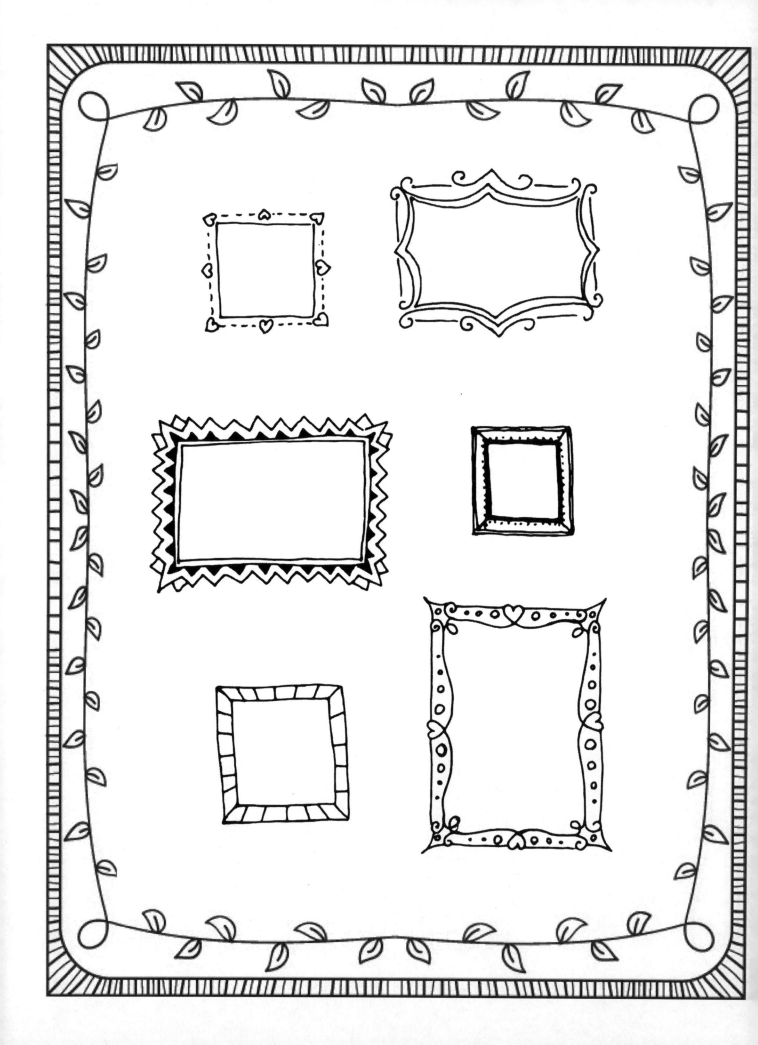

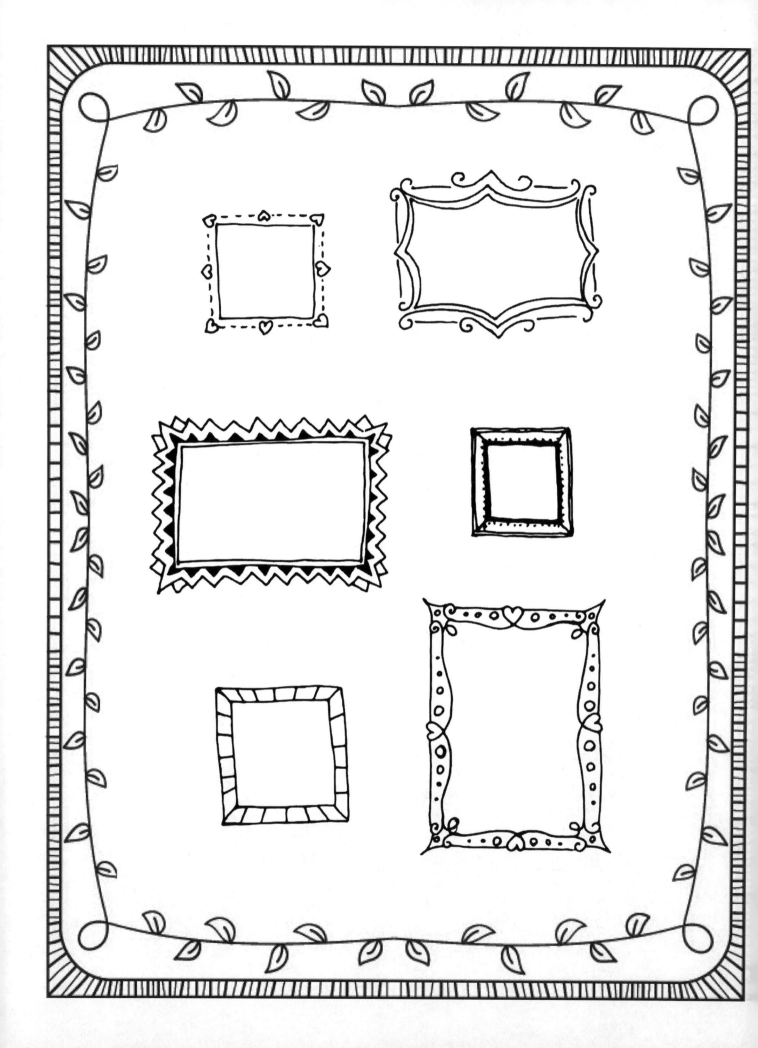

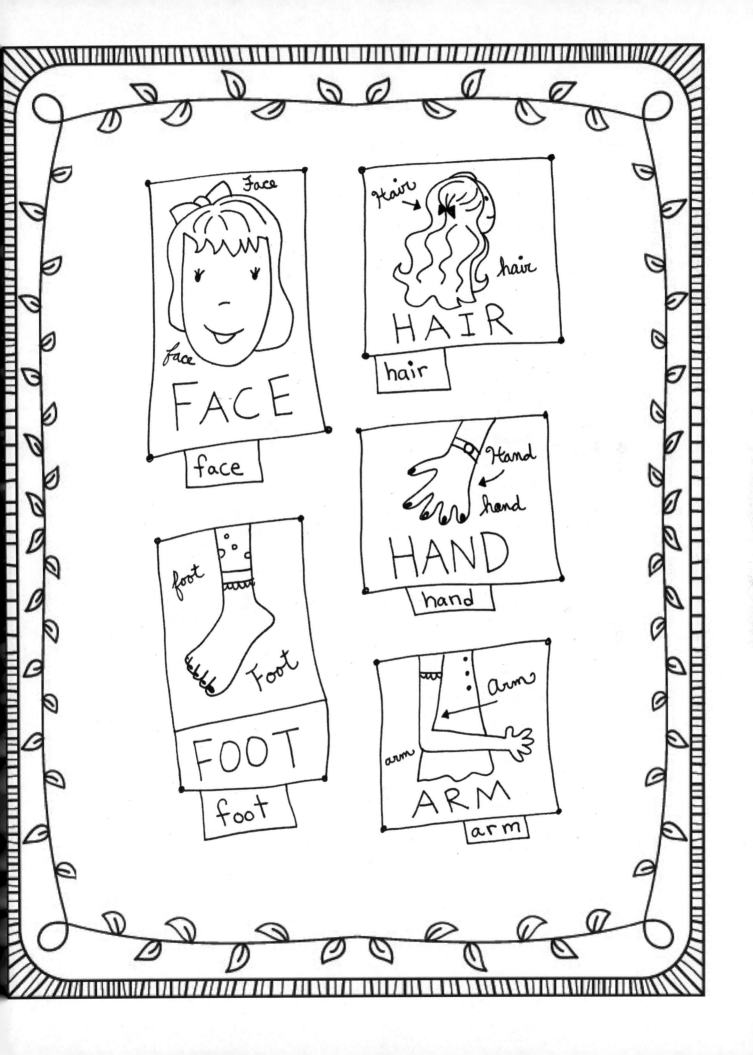

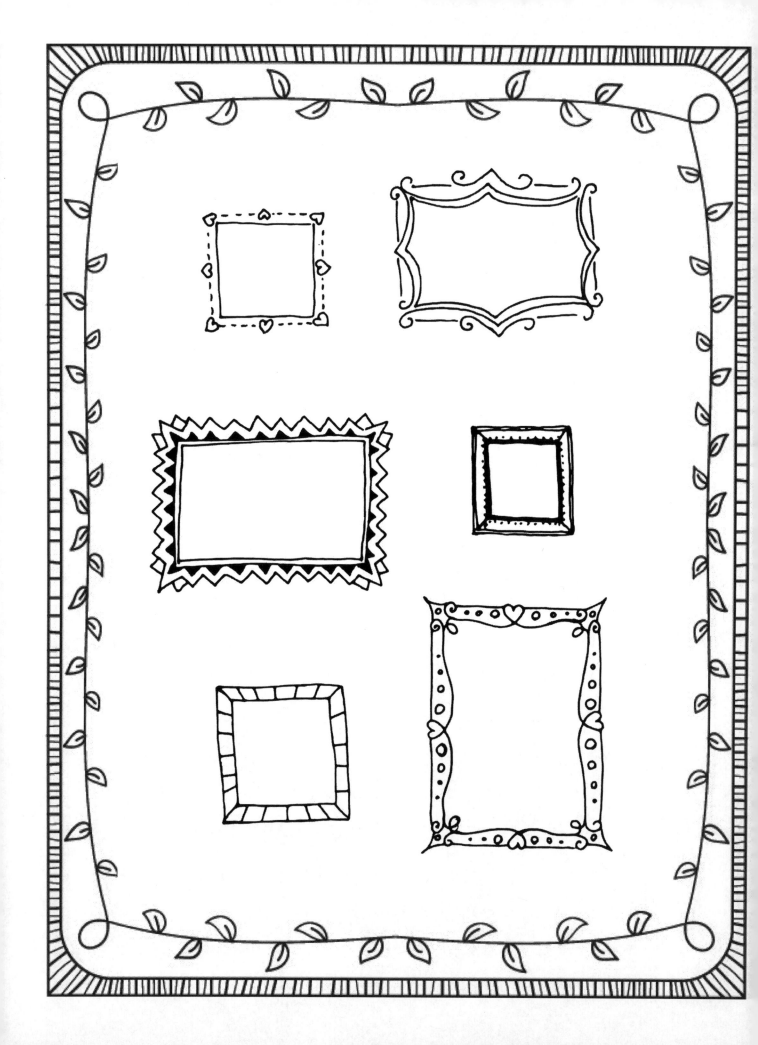

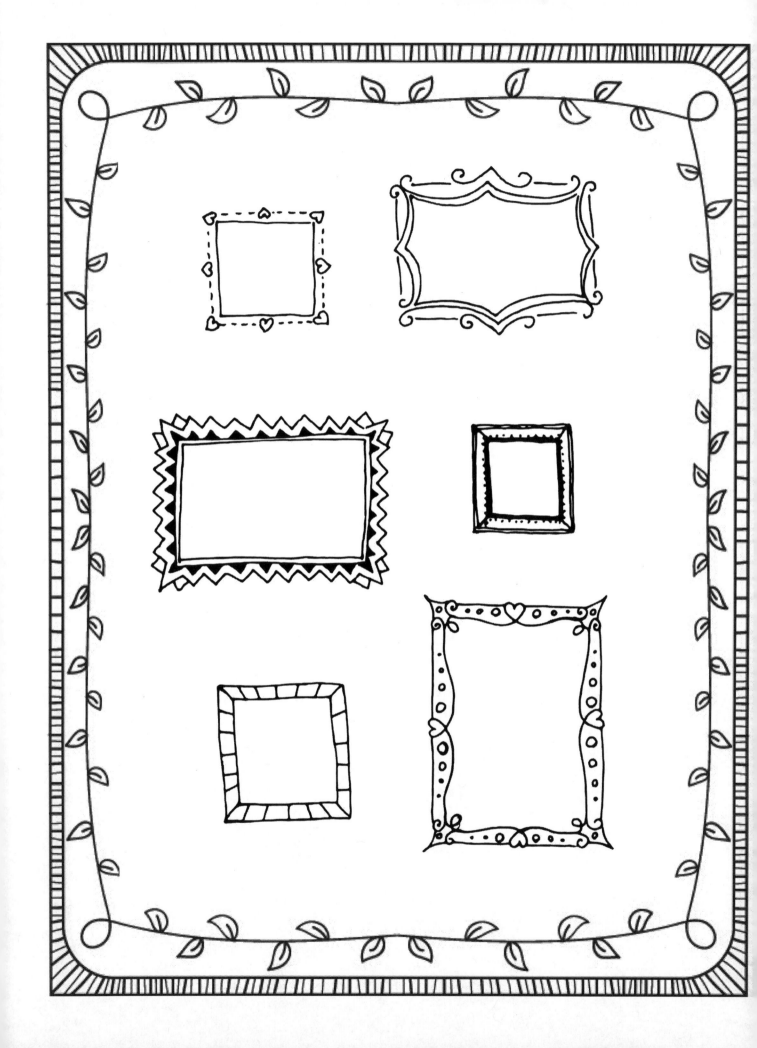

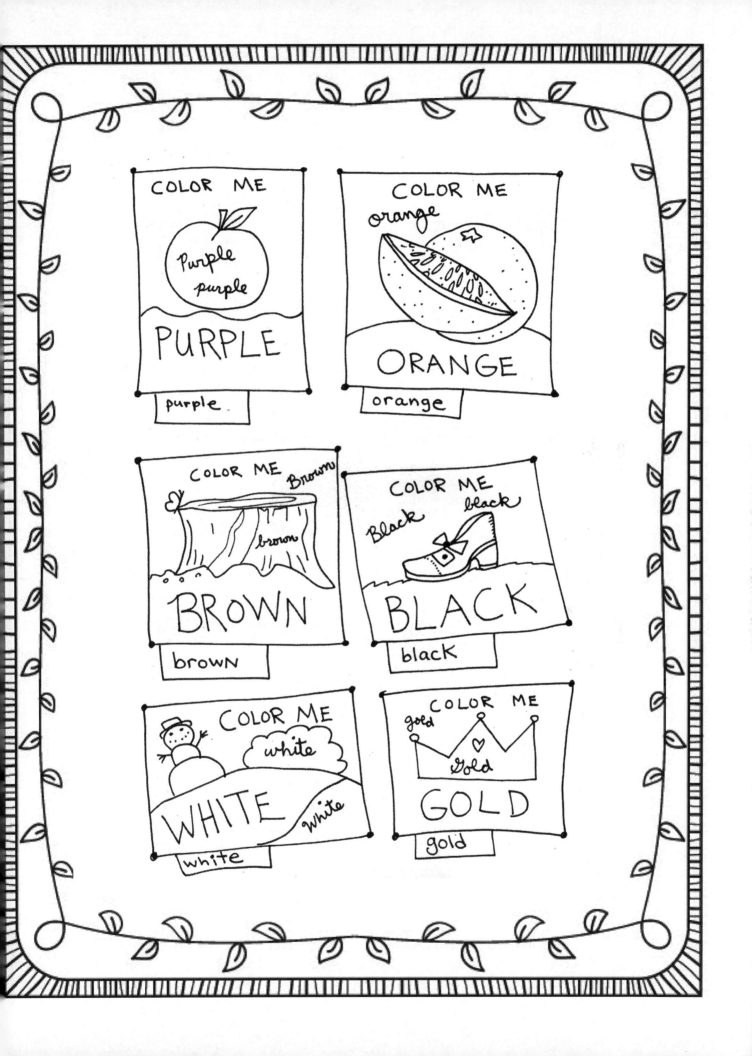

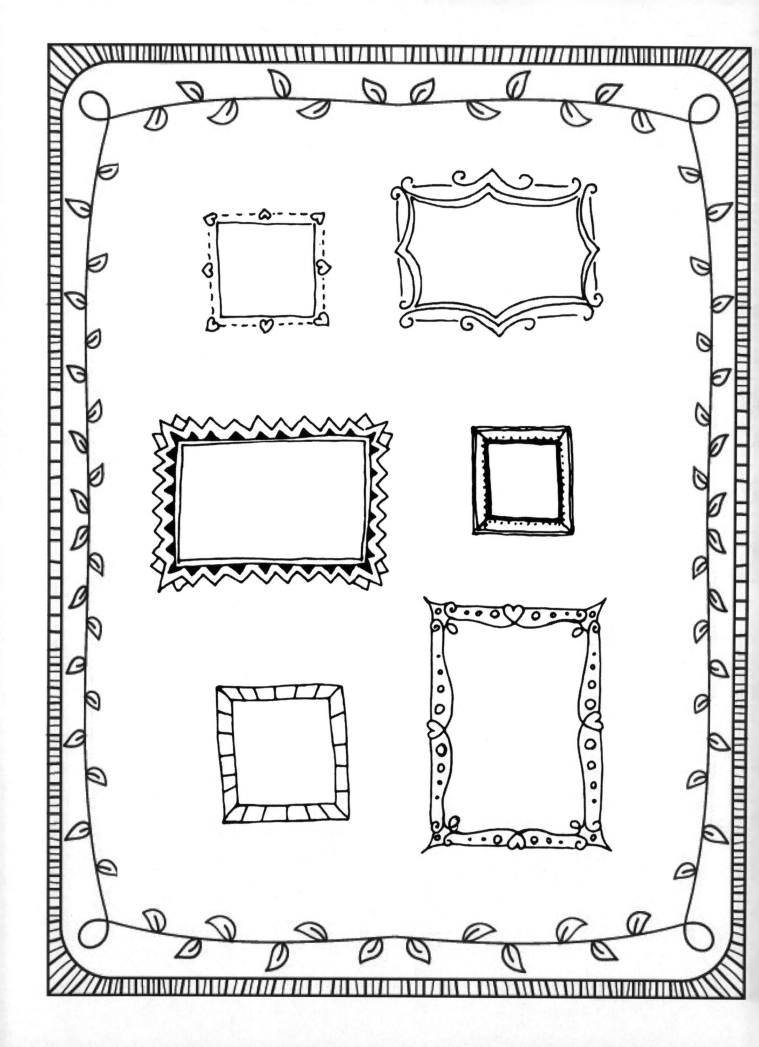

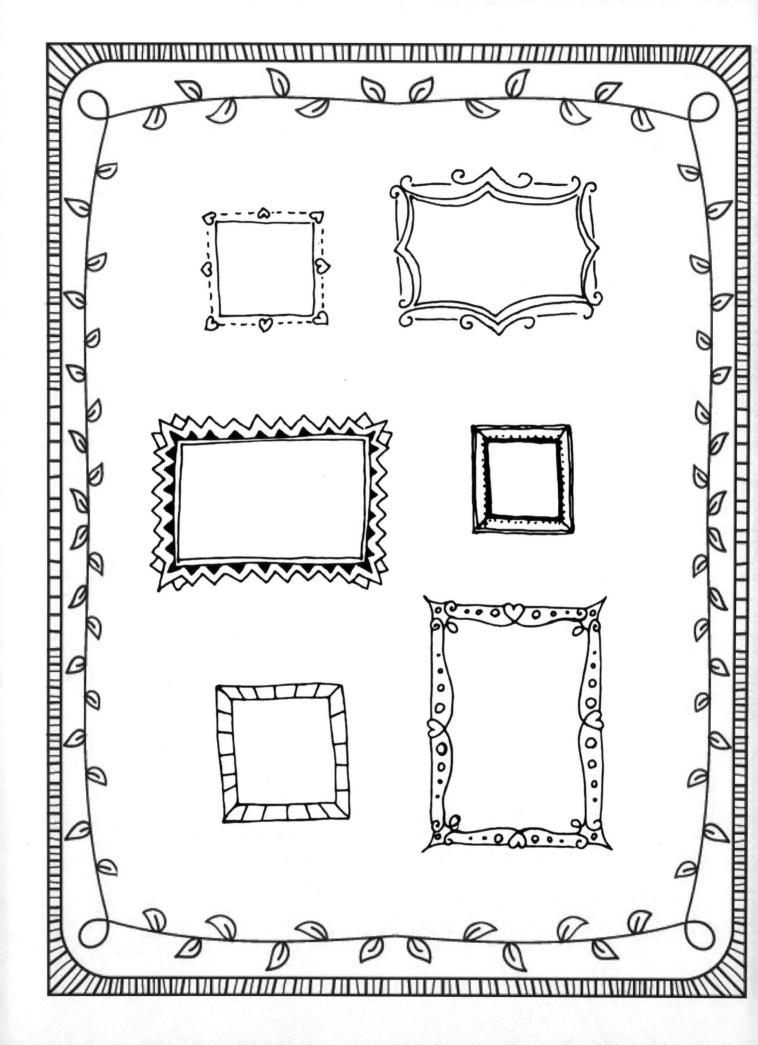

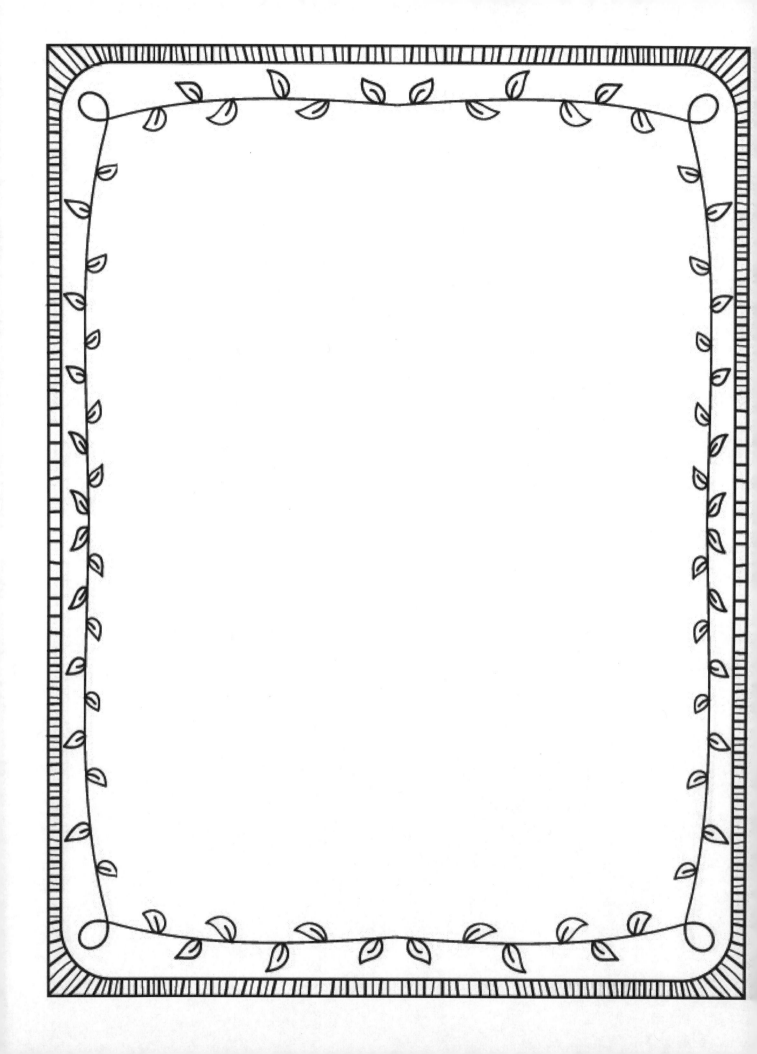

Made in United States
Orlando, FL
19 November 2024

54126024R00059